Steps To Passover

Dr. Akiva Gamliel Belk
Dean of Jewish Studies
B'nai Noach Torah Institute, LLC

Jewishpath.org
B'nai Noach Torah Institute, LLC
http://www.bnti.us

Copyright © 2016
Dr. Akiva Gamliel Belk
All rights reserved
ISBN – 13: 978-0692645109
ISBN - 10: 0692645101

Publisher
B'nai Noach Torah Institute, LLC,
POB 14 • Cedar Hill, MO 63016
First Edition 2016
636.543.8000

Table of Contents

Introduction..7
  Passover, the Holiday of Freedom...............7
Chapter One..17
  It Was Exactly Midnight............................17
Chapter Two...25
  Death Was Everywhere!..........................25
Chapter Three..33
  Chametz - What Is It?.............................33
Chapter Four..47
  Preparing For Passover..........................47
Chapter Five...53
  Passover Kitchen Preparation.................53
Chapter Six...61
  Relating to Your Children.......................61
Chapter Seven..65
  Purchasing Passover Food....................65
Chapter Eight...73
  Selling, Searching And Burning Chometz..73

Chapter Nine...81
   Haggadahs And Jewish Tradition...............81
Chapter Ten...87
   The Seder Plate..87
Chapter Eleven..93
   Wine..93
Chapter Twelve...97
   The Four Cups Of Wine..........................97
Chapter Thirteen..101
   Telling The Passover Story....................101
Chapter Fourteen.......................................107
   How To Count the Omer 107
Chapter Fifteen..113
   The Passover Offering............................113
Chapter Sixteen...123
   The Four Questions................................123
Chapter Seventeen.....................................127
   The Matzah Bake 127
About The Author......................................137
Books By Dr. Akiva Gamliel Belk...............139

Introduction

Passover, the Holiday of Freedom

It would be nice if this book helps us find more meaning and understanding about Passover[1] and Passover Observances. That is my goal. Most of us have some Observances associated with Passover. This book is intended to fill in the blanks for individuals with limited knowledge of Passover Observances like me many years ago.

I remember back to my first Passover experience in 5731 From Creation[2] that was in 1971. I knew it was close to Passover but wondered, how does one observe Passover. I was raised with a heavy Christian influence.

---

1 Passover פֶּסַח Pesach / Passover is The Word used to describe the Angel of Death Passing over The Homes in Egypt that had lamb or kid's blood on the door post. The Lord God Required the blood on the doorpost to protect the firstborn of the household. The blood ONLY protected the firstborn. See Exodus 12.

2 All dates mentioned in this book are counted from The Biblical counting which begins at creation, i.e. 0000 From Creation.

Jewish Observances had faded. Unfortunately it is not unusual these days. At that Time, I was stationed aboard a US Naval vessel moored to the dock in another country. At that time, I thought long and hard about how to observe Passover. Somehow I knew Kosher wine was part of Passover. That is where I started. I went to the enlisted men's lounge on base and found a place to be seated. The waitress came to my table. I asked if they had a bottle of Mogan David. She answered, 'wait and I'll check.' After a long time, she returned with an unopened bottle of Mogan David. I explained that I was Jewish and wanted to celebrate Passover. I requested a paper cup. After paying for the bottle and leaving a tip, I disappeared into the night. Where was I to go? How could I celebrate Passover? I didn't know. I remember walking down to the end of what appeared to be a fishing pier and sitting down on the old wooden pier opening the brown paper sack with the bottle of Mogan David wine in it and saying a simple prayer. My prayer went something like this: O Lord, I don't know how to celebrate Passover but realize I need to do something. What is it? I was like the simple child in our Seder Haggadah³. I took the bottle of wine and said, Oh Lord, please bless this wine in Jesus Name Amen! Obviously, I didn't understand the issues with Judaism and Jesus. This was my first Passover. I was doing the best a wandering Jew could without a Teacher. I poured wine into the paper cup and took a drink of the wine. I thought, Wow! Mogan David is really sweet.

As I drank the wine my thoughts returned to the Children of Israel being delivered from Egypt and about my mother and father may they rest in peace. Without realizing it, I was mentally reviewing the story of deliverance. I was retelling the story of liberation, which is one of the purposes for the Seder Meal.⁴ As the

---

3 Haggadah הַגָדָה means telling. The Haggadah is a short book that establishes the order of the Passover Seder Meal. When we drink wine and enjoy the festivities of the Seder Meal. The Haggadah helps us to stay on track. We follow the steps in the Haggadah so we carefully Observe the Mitzvot of telling the story to our children.

4 Seder Meal - In Jewish homes a traditional meal is prepared for the first and second nights of Passover. This is called the Seder Meal or The Passover Seder. סֵדֶר Seder means order or arrangement. During the Seder meal we retell the story of The People of Israel's deliverance by The Mighty Hand of The Lord God from Egyptian slavery. 'And you

night drew on and the wine took hold. I felt like singing. Later, I learned shipmates in the bunk area were kept up by my night long croon. Hours later as the wine wore off I tried standing up. My head was swirling. Ohh I could not walk straight. How I made it back to the ship that evening is a mystery. I remember my Petty Officer First Class assisting me towards the tailgate then to my bunk. I remember a shipmate praying for me as I sang my heart out. When morning came, my head hurt.

That Observance was not exactly how Passover is celebrated, but some elements of Passover Observance were there.

Dear Reader, if you are somewhere around where I was, this book on the Steps To Passover will be helpful.

Years later, I began returning to Torah

---

shall tell your son in that day, saying, This is done because of that which the Lord did to me when I came forth out of Egypt, Exodus 13.8.

Observances. I was a Baal Teshuvah[5]. I rented an apartment in the Jewish Community and began trying to Observe The Mitzvot[6] of Ha Torah[7]. One of the very first things I learned about Passover is EXPENSE! We will discuss the expenses related to Passover later. Don't let the cost stand in your way. Observe what you can afford to observe. I understand that we may not be able to reach the highest level of observance. Still, we should attempt to reach a level of observance just a little beyond the previous year. We should try to challenge ourselves to do a little more. This shows a good pattern of growth and development year following year.

Each of us is on different levels of Observance. We begin where we are and try to improve.

---

5 Baal Teshuvah בַּעַל תְּשׁוּבָה means Master of Return. This is the name assigned to a Jew who returns from assimilation to Torah Observances.
6 Mitzvot מִצְווֹת Mitzvot is plural for Mitzvah מִצְוָה meaning Command, Law or Observance. The Lord God Gave Jewish People 613 Mitzvot to guide us.
7 HaTorah הַתּוֹרָה is The Five Books of Moses, Genesis Exodus, Leviticus, Numbers and Deuteronomy, The Pentateuch are The Torah. includes The Covenant and The 613 Mitzvot.

Certain events proceed Passover. Leading up to Passover housecleaning, auto cleaning, office cleaning and so forth are necessary to rid ourselves of Chometz.[8] I believe the term 'Spring Cleaning' began with Passover Observance.

When I say Torah Observance of Passover, I am making reference to the Torah's Interpretation of how Passover is to be observed. I am making reference as to how The People of Israel have been observing Passover for 3500 years.

Passover is known as the 'Festival of Freedom' because The Lord God delivered three million Jews from hard murderous slavery in Egypt. So we will focus some on the attitude of freedom. What does it feel like to be free? Leading up to

---

[8] Chometz חָמֵץ Chometz is the process that causes leavening or fermenting. Liquid is added to one of the five grains. After 18 minutes, leavening or fermenting begin. Any product that includes includes one of the five grains as an ingredient may have leavening or fermenting. During Passover we are not to consume products that have fermented. We cannot consume products with leaven. Therefore we clean everywhere to remove the Chometz. We gather our Chometz together and sell it to non-Jews.

Passover and during Passover we are in the season of freedom. We face our struggles, our habits, our problems, our addictions with renewed commitment to acknowledge and to conquer them. We do Teshuvah.⁹ We also call Teshuvah, shuvah. We are only responsible for things within our boundaries.

When we consider freedom, we consider turning over a new leaf. We consider adjusting how we live. We consider shuvah.

When The Lord commanded Moses to go to Egypt Jacob and all of his sons were dead. The men of leadership, the men of wisdom, and the men of God's direct revelation were gone. Jacob's grandchildren were being forced into slavery. Parents and children were raised as slaves. They had a slave mentality. They knew nothing else! Individuals who were raised with a particular ideology, religion, culture without being exposed to other possibilities may, in

---

9   Teshuvah תְּשׁוּבָה meaning, to repent, to return, to the correct path. To repent we acknowledge our mistake, we make a plan to not repeat our mistake, we offer restitution to those we have injured. We do an about face. We return to The Path of Right Living given to us in Ha Torah.

fact, have blinders on. Seeking The Truth requires removing our blinders. Removing blinders is a form of freedom.

It was in this situation that The Lord God Commanded Moshe to go to Egypt to begin the process of delivering His people from the bonds of slavery. This was not an easy task. There were millions of people who hated slavery but who lack the ability to free themselves. Similar situations exist today! We have billions of people who want to know The Truth, who want a clear revelation of God. Many are searching. Are they prepared for what they will discover?

Our world needs a deliverer. Our world needs a deliverer who will untangle all the world's religions, beliefs, and problems. The day of freedom is coming!! However, until that day of total freedom comes we have the responsibility of using the tools available to us to free us. Passover is where we begin.

Passover teaches us that God does the

revealing. Passover leads us through the struggles of our slavery to deliverance and freedom. The Lord God has heard our cries for freedom. He Sees our desires to be free from those issues that bother and imprison us. We must participate. Passover teaches us the steps to freedom. It's not as simple as walking away from the slave camps that have a hold on us. Every Passover requires us to remember our struggle for freedom. Passover reminds us there are disappointments! During the one year struggle to leave Egypt Moses experienced times when he felt really low. He often experienced the feelings of failure after sparring with Pharaoh. He experienced feelings of rejection from The People of Israel who suffered under a greatly increased workload.

How does our position in life affect our cries to The Lord? What are our expectations? Do we anticipate more because we are great, because we are righteous, because we are rich? Does our position of righteousness, strength, and wealth give us a false sense of God's responsibility to us? Are we expecting nothing from The Lord because we feel low, because we do not appear to be on a high level of righteousness, because we do not seem to be great, because we are poor? Has our lack of self-esteem clouded our perception of God? Do we feel so low, so unworthy that our mind develops a negative expectation from God?

Chapter One
It Was Exactly Midnight

The tension had been escalating for years. Feelings of resentment were at an all-time high. Friction filled the air. Cooperation was at an all-time low. People were gathering in small pockets throughout the entire country. The talk of freedom was everywhere. Among the ruling party, there were many factions. The indifferent said, 'Let them go, they are nothing but trouble! Look at all the misfortune over this past year.'

Staunch party members felt, 'The government needs to step in and make a stand! Enough of this rebellion! Teach them a lesson they won't forget!'

The liberals denounced the administration, 'Rebellion! Anarchy! Terrorism! What do you expect from the working class? Their living conditions are so congested with all the children. They're like insects. They're everywhere! They need better housing, more free time, a few days to cool their jets in the hot desert sun.'

The religious party of Egypt used this opportunity as a forum to attract new members. It was clear from their view that 'the gods were very angry.' They went from house to house, street to street throughout the entire country proclaiming their doomsday message, 'The world is coming to an end! Let the working class go! The God of the working class is angry! Their God is warring with our gods...'

The intellectual class called on government members to renew peace accords with influential leaders of the working class. 'Certainly something could be worked out if the ruling class and the working class would just sit down and talk...'

Tensions had only increased during the past year since the return of Moses, an exiled holy man, formerly of the ruling class. Union bosses jumped at the opportunity to support this charismatic leader of the grassroots civil rights organization called 'Free My People.'
The working class throughout the country joined making outrageous demands. Months earlier, they rioted and danced in the streets setting the entire country on fire. It was like stones of fire fell from the heavens. Several reporters stated, 'It was hellfire falling from the sky.' Crops were burned, buildings leveled. The country was declared a disaster area except for Goshen County, which surprisingly remained unscathed.

Many of the working class attributed great miracles to the leader of FMP movement. The government issued many denials. When the waters of the Nile turned red with blood, the working class said their leader had smitten the waters. The government issued a denial stating scientists working in conjunction with the National Weather Service were on record for years warning that such an unusual phenomenon could happen under certain conditions. They also issued statements about the frogs and the lice and the death of cattle which resulted from the Nile turning red.

The working class, on the other hand, accredited their leader with the supernatural power of bringing on these national tragedies.

The ruling class was becoming increasingly more skeptical with the government's denials, especially their latest. No one was buying the government's explanation that the terrifying darkness had gripped the entire country because the sun god was angry.

A growing number of the ruling class were very fearful of Moshe and his brother Aharon, leaders of FMP! An increasingly large number were openly acknowledging their fear over his latest proclamation called, 'First Death.' These fears were heightened yesterday when members of the working class throughout the country gathered young lambs for a ritual slaughter to take place on the 14th of the month.

The entire country was in an uproar! The government seemed powerless to stop this uprising of the working class. Government leaders were demanding that this revolt be put down immediately. Members of the government who were known worshipers of the lamb god were angry and very outspoken! Debates are expected to continue late into the night...

In anticipation of the government crushing this revolt and ordering a nationwide curfew on the 14th the General of the army of Egypt ordered all inactive members to report immediately stating, 'All soldiers of the mighty army of Egypt will be on active duty to enforce the curfew.' He denied numerous reports that many members were refusing to stay and that many active members had deserted!

As government breakdown continued, the ruling class began offering appeasement to the working class with gold, silver, jewels, art and great wealth. The entire country was in disarray!! The working class, in direct defiance of the government, began slaughtering thousands of lambs and placing the lambs' blood on their doorposts...

There is enormous fear that many of the ruling class are attempting to flee the country in defiance of the curfew. Soldiers are posted on the roads to turn them back... Darkness is approaching as the fear mounts... Night comes....

Then... it... was... exactly... midnight...

Dear Reader, holy reader, one can only imagine what it must have been like for those living in Egypt during the months, weeks, days and even hours leading up to the tenth and final plague when The Children of Israel would be driven out...

Chapter Two
Death Was Everywhere!

Wow! Can you believe it? We are free! We are really FREE!

Great destruction happened yesterday. Death was in the air! Everywhere in Mitzriam! Bitter cries and wailing were everywhere. Dead soldiers, dead people and dead animals were everywhere. Our deliverance was so great! Baruch Hashem! God was so powerful! Blessed is His Name! May He be Blessed forever! After 430 years of slavery it came to an abrupt end. Thank God! I didn't know if it ever would! Like every Jew here, I was dearly hoping our slavery would end! It did! Thank God! It's amazing! It's over! Am I alive? Pinch me! It happened so quickly... so very quickly. Word spread that we were leaving. It was for real! We only had time to prepare a little Matzoh, unleavened bread! Then soldiers were all over us. "Get your things!" Get Out! Leave this country! Get out!" Echoes of their harsh commands could be heard for blocks as Jews rushed by our home with their families, cattle and great wealth. We also rushed to join our leader Moshe even before the soldiers arrived.

It was like day in the dark of night. This huge fire lit up the entire sky. Moshe, our leader, and director of Free My People stood off a little distance from the Fire as B'nei Yisroel continued to join him.

It was actually happening! The ruling class were leaning out their windows and screaming as we passed by, "Get out of our country! My son is dead because of you.. My father... My sister!" The impact of death was so great. People were running through the streets out of their minds! People sped by on horses and in chariots towards the homes of relatives and friends surveying the impact of death!

There is no way to explain the power of death. Parents holding their dead children weeping bitterly as we passed by. Children bending over dead mothers, fathers, siblings. Yes, there was enormous grief.

And then there was our great, vast exultation. It was impossible for us to lend even small feelings of compassion towards those who had brutally murdered, raped and beaten us for years. They were everywhere as we left! The vengeance of God was everywhere! Baruch Hashem!

We could not contain ourselves seeing so many of our enemies lying dead before us... It was such an overwhelming feeling... Emotions bottled up for years erupted as we rushed from Mitzriam! The army was devastated. They were muddled! It was difficult for them to function. Many of their leaders were dead. Disarray, chaos and all forms of confusion were happening all around us. That was yesterday...

The Fire began to move. It led us. All B'nei Yisroel followed. Those in the back could see just as those in the front, close to the Fire. No one was cold. The Fire regulated the temperature throughout all B'nei Yisroel.

The Fire was so bright that one had to look off a great distance to realize it was actually night. Eventually dawn came. The Fire transformed into this huge, soft, fluffy, massive Cloud as the sun began to rise. The Cloud blocked the sun from beating down on us as we traveled.

No one experienced exhaustion! It was very comfortable. We stopped to eat and set up camp at Sukkos after putting distance between Mitzriam and us. Tomorrow we are planning on journeying on to Eisom at the edge of the desert.

Tonight we sit at our own campfires as free people. Thank God! The Fire lights the sky again. It's magnificent! It's indescribable! Our leader Moshe listens to the Fire. The Fire tells him what to do. He does what the Fire says! Moshe explained to our leaders that God is the Fire by night and God is the Cloud by day. This is really incredible!! In my wildest considerations I could never have imagined something like this!

We are so happy! We are Free! Thank God, we are Free! No one will be able to sleep tonight. Stories are all over our camp about the Mighty Hand of God delivering us! Our children are laughing, really laughing! Everyone is so incredibly joyful! Baruch Hashem! We dreamed of this day! Now, it's here! Thank God! Wow! This feeling of freedom is so powerful! I can't describe it!

Just yesterday we were slaves! We were the despised working class in Mitzriam! Our lives were in jeopardy, God forbid! The army of Mitzriam, the greatest army in the world, was making preparations to destroy us, God forbid! ... to end our struggle for freedom, God forbid! Yet tonight we sit here in Sukkos around campfires as free people! If we can go to bed tonight we will go to bed as free people for the first time in our lives.

Even Jochaved, Moshe's mother, who was born between the gates as our father Yaakov came to join Yosief and to spare our family, enjoys freedom tonight after enduring 210 years in Mitzriam and 116 years of slavery and struggle for freedom...

Thank God, the bones of Yosief are with us tonight! We will bury them, God willing, in the land of promise!

Wow! Can you believe we are free? Really Free?

Dear Reader, holy reader, you can join us in the Festival of Freedom. You can share in the gift of freedom. Every year we remember and honor Hashem for delivering us from the bitter slavery in Mitzriam. This year you can join in our celebration. Shuvah is the path to freedom. Returning to God is the path of freedom! Pursue freedom by returning to God! At least come closer to God! Even a little closer is good and a lot is better!

We do this by identifying our sins! We do this by acknowledging our mistakes. We take full ownership of errors. We own our sins! We did them! They belong to us! It was our choice! Then we separate ourselves from our errors, from our sins! We are here. Our sins and our errors are there. Next we determine not to go over there. Over where? Over there where our sins and error are. We stop visiting them. We move away from them. We leave them behind! We join the Festival of Freedom! We remember how we were slaves to our sins, to our errors, but now, thank God, we are free!

Chapter Three

Chametz - What Is It?

There are two sides to living. There is living during Passover and there is living throughout the rest of the year. The two times for living are represented by Matzah and Chametz. Matzah has no leaven, i.e. yeast. Matzah is simply water and flour. Matzah is normally dry and hard having a plain taste. Matzah represents the time of the year when we humble ourselves. We restrain our ego. We try to bring our homes to a high level of santification. We labor to purify ourselves from pride. We try to raise our spiritual level. We live in the Matzah world eight days each year.

The Chametz world has leaven. Chametz is tastey. Chametz is puffy and with some pride.

Exodus 13.7   Shares a unique Observance,

which ONLY relates to Passover. We, The People of Israel are required to Observe this Command for a little over a week each year. The Command is one of the 613 Observances written in Ha Torah.

'The Lord spoke to Moshe Saying, Matzot must be eaten during these seven days. And no chametz may be seen in your possession, and no leaven may be seen within any of your boundaries,' Exodus 13.7.

The word chametz means to become sour, leavened, fermented. Chametz describes the process which occurs by just adding liquid to any of the five-grain products.[10] When liquid is added, after a short time, i.e. 18 minutes or longer the grain begins to ferment. Once the grain begins to ferment, it is chametz. Any utensil, appliance, counter, table, floor, wall or sink that touches chametz becomes contaminated by the chametz. Sometimes that

---
10 The five grains are wheat, barley, oats, rye and spelt.

contamination can be corrected. Sometimes it cannot. This is what chametz is.

Chametz is found in many kosher food products. That is why we use the special designation, KOSHER FOR PASSOVER or KOSHER La PASSOVER. During this short period surrounding Passover. It is very important to make this distinction so we do not violate the Torah Commandment 'no chametz may be seen in your possession and no leaven may be seen within any of your boundaries.'

What does this mean? How are we to react to this Command? Dear Reader, we are to cleanse our homes and ourselves for Passover. Most of us accomplish this by dividing our home into areas for Passover cleaning. Jews must do all that they can to remove the chametz which includes the bread crumbs, the cookie crumbs, the cake crumbs, the pie crumbs, the candy, the snacks, from everywhere in their homes. This also means one must read many labels to determine if any form of chametz exists in food, health product, cleaning product. One must also determine if the product is manufactured according to the stricter standards of Passover. The easiest way is to make sure a product is labeled Kosher for Passover.

I am not saying this is fun, but it can be fun. It's all in how we approach Passover cleaning.

Several years back we learned that the Rebbetzin had cancer and would require four surgeries along with chemotherapy. The news was devestating. The Rebbetzin began the process. It was very difficult. The Rebbetzin was forced to take time from work yet she returned to work just a couple of days after the first surgery. Working was fatiguing. The Rebbetzin worked from home. She worked for a few hours then rested, then she worked more. It was arduous!! During that eighteen month time we went to over 180 medical treatments, doctor appointments etc. It was so trying. We kept our Sabbath meals simple. We did not have visitors during this time. The Rebbetzin was so ill. Revi fought to live. Revi fought to hold her head high.

Passover was approaching. One evening Revi called me to her bedside and said, 'Honey what are we going to do?' I didn't know. Later I spoke with a woman who does house cleaning to see if she would be available to help us with our house cleaning. She told me her price. I said fine. We went over the details. She agreed to help with our house cleaning. I scheduled her for several days of cleaning. The day she was to begin she didn't show up. Perhaps she phoned with some excuse but I don't recall her phoning. I drove to her place of work to speak with her. She said something came up. In addition she would not be able to clean the second day either. I explaind the importance of her being dependable and how important this house cleaning was. We rescheduled for the next week. It would be hetic. The only time she had available was the day before Passover in the afternoon and the day Passover began. The first seder meal would be that night. It was in the late afternoon the day before Passover when our phone rang. Again, something came up. She couldn't come. . . I had already phoned individuals and companies that did house cleaning. Some did not return our calls. Some would not come into our area. Some were already scheduled. Some were too expensive.

It is good that several weeks before I began some Passover cleaning but the house was nowhere near the Rebbetzin's level of cleaning. I was frantic! It was necessary to immediately stop everything. I immediately returned to cleaning our home. Before long I heard a banging and clanging. It was the Rebbetzin. She rose to the occassion. In her weak frail and sick condition she began cleaning our home. She worked hard. She was determined!! She said, With God's help our home will be ready for Passover. Thank God our home was ready. We did our best. We we were thankful to enjoy Passover together.

Preparing for Passover can have unique challenges and some twists and turns. We do the best we can and go forward.

Let's discuss Passover cleaning for a few pages. When we clean our home it is important to know that some products in our homes which are labeled Kosher for Passover may not be kosher for Passover!! How can this be? What could cause this? A simple example of this is an opened bag of sugar that one may have used a spoon or cup to scoop sugar out of. While the sugar may be kosher for Passover, the spoon, and the cup are not. What is the rule regarding this situation? How do we handle this? Once a bag or container is opened - even if nothing has been used to scoop the product out - it is at that point considered chametz. It is considered chametz because it has been opened and used in an area not kosher for Passover!

Why do I say, in an area 'not kosher for Passover'? Readers, any area that all chametz has not been removed from and then cleaned is not kosher for Passover. Remember even cleaning products must be 'Kosher for Passover.' Think about this. Here are some examples to consider. The beautiful Shabbat candleholders used every Shabbat by the lady of the house to enter into Shabbat are not kosher for Passover. They must be put away or be kashered for Passover. The same applies to the Siddurim, i.e. prayer books that we use during the week and on Sabbath. The same applies to the bentshers, i.e. the little books that we say blessings from after we conclude a meal. The challah board, the challah cover, the challah knife, the Kiddish cup, the Shabbat plates, dishes, knives, silverware, glasses, pots, pans, etc. are not kosher for Passover unless unless one has specially kashered them for Passover. Many cannot be kashered for Passover.

Readers, I learned the laws of Passover from some great Torah Teachers like the Hornosteipler Rebbe, Ha Rav Rabbi Mordecai Twerski whose genealogical dynasty reaches back to Bible times. I learned with Ha-Rav

Rabbi Dovid Nussbaum of Yeshiva Toras Chaim Beit Medrash, Ha-Rav Rabbi Yaakov Meyer. I have worked as a mashgiach, i.e. rabbinic supervisor} for such organizations as Union of Orthodox Jewish Congregations, Tri Salom, Vad Hakashrus, etc. So please listen.

One cannot use everyday utensils and dishes at Passover! The Lord placed Passover on a much higher level. Each year we are reminded of this. One of the very special purposes of Passover is to do a thorough housecleaning at Passover and to do the very same spiritually!

Earlier I stated that some items can be kashered for Passover. Any item made of 100% metal can be kashered for Passover. It cannot have plastic or wooden handles. It must be 100% metal or completely metal plated! Cloth items that can be washed, like tablecloths or napkins, can be kashered for Passover.

It was about three weeks before Passover. This was the day The Rav's Community Kosher For Passover Project began. Members of the Robbie's staff gathered. We began by cleaning a space where we would set up our Kosher For Passover Keilim[11] boiling station. We kashered everything in the kitchen and other rooms. After removing the chametz we went to the storage area where our Kosher for Passover Items were stored. We removed those items. We set up a work table and a propane gas stove for the explicit purpose of boiling a large pot of water. The pot would hold perhaps 16 gallons of water. During our santification of Kosher pots, pans, utensils, silverware etc. it was necessary for the water to remain boiling.

The purpose for this special service was to assist members of our community in correctly preparing keilim for Passover. The entire Jewish Community was invited to come use our service. The environment was non threatening.

---

11 כַּלִים Kah Leem / Keilim meaning pots, pans utensils etc.

In part our purpose was to assist individuals who wanted to use kosher keilim they used with chametz throughout the year to be able to use at Passover. We inspected keilim to determine if they could be koshered for Passover. We asked questions. We taught. It was really special! Our goal was to connect with people in our community. Our goal was to share about Judaism. Our goal was to reach out.

Some items could not be kaushered for Passover. Some items required more cleaning. On some, keilim handles were removed. Everything had to first be prepared then boiled. We boiled the items that could be kashured because boiling water kills, i.e. destroys the chametz.

Offering this service allowed individuals to use special itmes at Passover that they enjoyed using throughout the year. Some individuals could not afford to purchase new pots, pans, silverware etc. Our service helped them to us some of what they already owned. Glass and plastic items used throughout the year could not be kashured for Passover. Some individuals needed to purchase items used especially for Passover.

We are told, Three times a year you are to celebrate with Me, Hashem, You must keep the Festival of מַצּוֹת Matzot. You must eat matzot for Seven Days as I have Commanded you. This Festival must be celebrated at the appointed time, during The Month when the grain is ripened, for it is at this time you went out of Egypt... You must not sacrifice while חָמֵץ chometz is present, Exodus 23:14-18

Our Sages say that חָמֵץ chometz represents sin. Leaven / yeast is the active ingredient that causes the dough to rise. When the dough rises, it becomes puffed up. The effect of chometz is compared to puffiness, haughtiness, and pride. The puffed up dough represents sin! We are warned about pride by Shlomo Ha-Melech. He said, 'Pride precedes destruction and arrogance comes before failure,' Proverbs 16:18.

We see this pride in the final letter of חָמֵץ chometz. The ץ Tzaddi is raised up.

Our sages say that matzoh represents sinlessness. Matzoh is 100% sin free. Matzoh has no leaven / yeast in it. The effect of this is humility, meekness and being unpretentious. We see this in the example of Moshe Rabbeinu, who was considered a very humble / meek man. We see this humility in the center letter of מַצּוֹת matzoh. The צ Tzaddi is lower and not raised up.

How do we rid ourselves of chometz? Immediately after Purim many Jews begin a room by room, special Passover cleaning of their homes garages, autos and businesses. We begin with the least used rooms first. We vacuum floors; move furniture; clean closets;

check every box, container and article of clothing for any chometz. Then we secure the room until Pesach. We do about one room a week until Pesach.

This is why I asked questions like, How many rooms do you have in your house, apartment, etc.? Count every room, bathroom, closet, porch, entrance way, storage areas, garage, etc. Why? It is best to plans in advance of Passover so we will be ready when Passover arrives.

It is much better to begin Passover cleaning sooner rather than later. This spreads the responsibility out and lessens the stress. We can carefully box and seal certain dry foods, canned foods, drinks, soaps, deodorants, etc. that are not kosher for Passover. We can place them in a designated area for sold items until after Passover. We sell all the chometz to a non-Jew before Passover. After Passover, we buy these items back. Every kitchen requires special preparations.

Chapter Four
Preparing For Passover

In the previous chapter be began discussing Passover cleaning. Passover is the season of cleansing. Some term this time as Spring Cleaning. This is a time for purifying our body soul and mind. Most individuals look at this season as a time of purify one's home from leaven[12]. The Midrash[13] Teaches us that there is also a time for separating from those who are assimilated. During the first three days of the ninth plague, i.e. the plague of darkness those who were assimilated among The People of Israel died[14]. Rashi Teaches that 4/5ths of The People of Israel died and were buried during

---

12 Exodus 12.19 - Seven days shall there be no leaven found in your houses; for whoever eats that which is leavened, that soul shall be cut off from the congregation of Israel, whether he is a stranger, or born in the land.
13 Midrash מִדְרָשׁ contains ancient Jewish Commentary, homiletic stories and interpretations of Hebrew Scripture.
14 Shemot Rabah 14.3 'There were transgressors in Israel who had Egyptian patrons and lived in affluence and honor who were unwilling to leave Egypt. So The Lord brought darkness upon the Egyptians for three days, so that The People of Israel could bury their unrighteous dead without their enemies seeing them.

the first three day span of darkness[15]. Our Sages Teach the announcement for the Ninth Plague was made on 15 Shevat[16] which is also known as The New Year For Trees. On Tu Bi'Shvat[17] we plant a tree in The Holy Land of Israel in the memory of a departed loved one. The Eleventh Month normally occurs during January in the Gregorian Calendar. This is a time of tearing away and a time of being torn away. The Torah does not permit Jews and non Jews to live as husband and wife. The Lord Comes to deliver us. Some of us do not want to be delivered. If we do not choose to separate on our own The Heavenly Court may separate between B'nei Yisroel[18] and B'nai Noach[19].

After nineteen years of marriage Passover 5753 From Creation would be very different. Our Family was experiencing division. I lived in a

---

15 'Rabbi Nosson Scherman, The Stone Edition The Chumash (Mesorah Publications, Ltd., Brooklyn, N.Y. 1993), p. 367
16 Rabbi Menachem M. Scheerson, Torah Chumash Devarim Kehot Publication Society (Brooklyn, NY 2011) p 63
17 Tu represents The Hebrew Letters ט Tet and ו Vav. The ט Tet equals nine. The ו Vav equals six. Together they equal fifteen. בִּשְׁבָט meaning in the eleventh.
18 בְּנֵי יִשְׂרָאֵל The children born to Jacob sons, i.e. the descendants of Israel.
19 B'nai Noach בְּנֵי נֹחַ The Children of Noah, i.e. the descendants of Noah and his wife, Na'amia.

small studio apartment where the neighbor next door and I shared the only bathroom. The rent was around $182.00 per month including electric, gas, water, sewer etc. The boys and their mother lived in the family home in the suburbs. The boys visited every other weekend.

It was especially difficult this year because we would not have our own Passover Seder. Joshua our older son would be with his mother. Joel our younger son would be with me sharing Passover as a guest of our Rabbi and his lovely family.

Before Passover it is necessary for those who are Jewish to clean their apartment, home, office, auto, etc. as best as they can to rid themselves of Chometz. That year I owned so little. Passover cleaning did not take much time. The kitchen area was about six feet wide by eight feet long. The bedroom area consisted of one chest of drawers and a single bed. The only closet was a small make shift closet several feet long and about eighteen inches deep. The living, dining area was small. The kitchen stove was a two burner stove. The oven was tiny. The Refrigerator was about nine cubic feet with a freezer the size of boot box. The kitchen table had several chairs. There was a lamp standing next to a front room chair. That's it.

Joel's cleaning assignment was the bedroom. My cleaning area was the kitchen. Joel and I made this deal. Any money in pants pockets or coats, under the bed in and around the dresser was Joel's if he found some. Joel found some change and maybe several dollars. To this day Joel claims I told him I lost a twenty dollar bill. I don't recall that. Perhaps Joel was making reference to an incident years earlier when I was a sailor. I lost $20.00 back then. Maybe we talked about this sailor story while driving from the family home to my studio apartment. I don't recall. How these type of things get twisted around only God Knows.

Joel did a really good job of Passover cleaning.

Joel expressed disappointment that he didn't find the $20.00. I asked, 'What Twenty Dollars?'

Joel replied, You know Dad, the Twenty dollars you lost.'

I said, 'Son, I didn't lose twenty dollars.'

Joel replied, 'Yes you did.'

I share this story about cleaning early in the book because one should plan to do a proper cleaning. Cleaning takes time based upon many factors. Our family cleans as many rooms like storage rooms, utility rooms, furnace rooms in advance of Passover and then seals them off until Passover. We begin with the least used rooms and narrow it down to the most used rooms the kitchen dining area and bathrooms.

Storage shelves in closets are cleaned and secured until Passover. Garages are cleaned. Autos are cleaned. We do what we can in advance of Passover to cleanse our homes of chometz.

The big cleaning is normally done first like blinds, curtains drapes, windows and walls etc.

Some families practice these policies all year that help to guard The Sabbath and High Holy Days. Pockets in Sabbath clothes like suit pants and jackets are sewed closed so nothing can be placed in them. This protects against carrying on The Sabbath and High Holidays. Parents teach children not to put any food items in pockets. Clothing is laundered before Passover begins. During Passover laundry is not done. Clothes that require dry cleaning remain in plastic until Passover begins.

Chapter Five

Passover Kitchen Preparation

Preparing the Kitchen for Passover is normally the final step of House Cleaning. The kitchen is the chametz center so it is the most challenging. Organizing the kitchen into sections works well for us. Every kitchen is different so it may be necessary to draw up a different plan. It is best to consult with the Community Rav with any questions or concerns about Passover, Passover cleaning, etc. There are many areas that cannot be made Kosher for Passover. We will discuss these first.

Porcelain Sink
The Porcelain Sink should be cleaned well but cannot be made Kosher for Passover. We cover the edges and interior of the sink with plastic or aluminum foil. We place new plastic wash tubs in our sink during Passover. We wash our dishes, silverware, pots and pans etc. in these

tubs. These may require changing several times.

Stainless Steel Sink
We clean the sink with Kosher for Passover soap and a New scrubbing sponge. We remove the sink drain stoppers. Most sink drain stoppers cannot be Kashured because they have a rubber stopper or are plastic. In our home we have the original sink drain stoppers that do not have a rubber bottom so we switch to that and Kasher it because it is all stainless steel. One can purchase new food stops for Passover if needed. Many individuals purchase a new pastic flat stopper for Passover or use a cloth to stop the sink. If you purchase a metal stopper remember to take to the Mikvah to Kosher it.

After the sink is cleaned some individuals use a bleach solution before pouring boiling water over the sink. When using any bleach solution please be careful to of eyes and surrounding area and use plastic gloves. The sink is now Kosher for Passover.

Dishwasher

Most diswashers cannot be made Kosher for Passover because their inside is plastic. The rolling racks are normally coated with plastic. Some dishwashers are stainless steel but the racks are plastic or plastic coated. Often the soap dispenser is plastic. In addition there are other plastic parts inside a diswasher.

Kosher Dishwasher Soap. Even if a dishwasher is 100 percent metal inside it may not be kosher for a number of reasons. Perhaps the dishwasher was used by someone else before purchasing the home. Perhaps Kosher dish washing soap was not used. We don't need to go into all the reasons. Its pretty clear that kashuring our dishwasher might be impossible. So what do we do? We can wash all our dishes by hand during Passover or we can follow a lenient observance. Remember our goal is to rid ourselves of chametz during Passover. The main place where chametz may gather is in filter and floor of the inside of the dishwasher. Make sure these are clean. Carefully inspect the rolling racks silverware trays for any food particles. Some individuals use a bleach solution protecting the eye with eye coverings and plastic gloves to wipe down the inside of the diswasher, rolling racks and silverware trays. Then we run the diswasher through a wash cycle using Kosher for Passover dish soap. This is a close as most of us can come to kaushering our dishwasher for Passover.

Refrigerator, Shelves, Glass and Drawer
Most refrigerators cannot be made totally kosher for Passover. The inside is normally plastic and glass which cannot be kashured. Our goal is to clean the refrigerator of chametz. We want to remove all food crumbs, drippings etc. We want our refrigerator 100 percent clean. All refrigerator should be cleaned. This is a good practice. Some individuals place all not kosher for Passover items in one refrigerator and seal it off untill Passover is over. The items in that refrigerator are sold as chametz to a non-Jew.

Individuals with one refrigerator will have items that are not kosher for Passover. We place these items in a box then seal the box. We set the box back in our clean refrigerator out of the way. The items in the box in the refrigerator are sold as chametz to a non-Jew.

The refrigerator freezer is a little more of a challenge. Most refrigerator freezers are frost free. Regardless, we remove all frozen items and wipe down the inside of the freezer. If necessary we defrost the freezer then wipe down the inside with soap and water. We remove ice trays. We replace ice trays with new ones after the freezer is cleaned. The ice maker is normally a self contained unit. Most individuals have no reason to open their Ice makers. It is normally chametz free. If there is any reason to think the ice maker may have chametz use plastic ice trays during Passover.

Stove Top, Range, Oven and Microwave
Again, Our goal is to cleanse our stove from all chametz. Each oven, stove range is different. I am going to limit my remarks to a gas stove and oven. We remove and clean the burner grates. Then we cover them with aluminum

foil. We clean around the burners. We clean the base the burner grates sit on then cover the base with aluminum foil. We clean the inside of our oven. We remove and clean metal racks. Then we cover them with foil. After the inside of our oven is clean and all racks have been secured we heat the oven to a high tempature for thirty minutes. Our Oven is now kosher for passover.

Most Microwaves require a good cleaning providing the microwave is kosher from date of purchase. After cleaning we place a paper towel in the glass microwave tray along with a cup of water. We run the microwave for three minutes. Then we wipe down the condensation. If anyone has concerns about the Microwave they should consult their community Rav or purchase a new Mixrowave for Passover.

We clean inside and outside of all cabinets. We clean under stoves and refrigerators. We clean the top of the referigrator. We clean light fixtures, window coverings, walls and ceilings. We clean tables, counter tops etc. Eventually we clean the floor.

The Order of Cleaning The Kitchen

We clean ceilings by dusting them. We scrub them when necesssary. We dust and wipe down walls. We wash curtains and clean blinds. We remove light domes to clean inside and outside. We dust ceiling fans then wipe them down. We work top to bottom. Then we turn our attention to establishing an area that is Kosher for Passover even though our kitchen is not yet kosher for Passover. We will need this area to lay items that have been cleaned. We will also need an area where we can place a few Kosher for Passover items like a tea pot or a Kosher pan we will use to boil water in.

The stove is cleaned first. The sinks are second. We move out from there. The Rebbetzin and I try to clean our referigrator shelves and oven racks outside when possible. When not possible we clean them in the sink then kashur the sink again. After everything has been cleaned and kashured to the best of our ability. This is different for each of us. We do our best.

Then we cover all counter tops, tables etc with plastic. We purchase plastic from a fabric store or department store.

After our kitchen is Koshered for Passover we bring our boxes out from the storage area and begin unloading them. We set up special plastic shelving which is only used for Passover. We place pots pans food, etc. on these shelves. This is our walk around pantry for Passover. Then the Rebbetzin begins the task of preparing the Pesach Seder Meal / The Passover Meal.

Dear Ones, it is easy to see how involved it maybe preparing the kitchen for Passover. It is best to try to have the kitchen prepared by early on the morning Passover begins.

Chapter Six

Relating to Your Children

Exodus 10.1 - 2
And The Lord spoke to Moshe, 'Come to Pharaoh, for I have strengthened [everything from Aleph to Tav of] his heart and [everything from Aleph to Tav of] his servants' hearts in order to [firmly] place these [powerful] signs in their midst.

And to relate [emphatically] in the ear of your son and son's son together that I made a mockery of Egypt and [from Aleph to Tav of powerful] signs that I performed among them so you will have the knowledge For I Am The Lord.

When one immerses themselves into these two verses, these 39 words, they discover a wealth of information. There are many sides to the Passover picture. One side is for fathers to relate and involve each child and grandchild in how The Lord made a mockery of Egypt.

Fathers, our responsibility is to know and relate how The Lord made a mockery of Egypt with miracles and powerful signs to deliver The People of Israel. We must relate the story of deliverance in such a way that it can be tasted. We must paint the picture like we are there right now!

In the above Scriptures, Ha Torah places the emphasis on 'fathers' and sons. Mothers and daughters are not omitted. Their presence and participation are understood. Mothers and daughters are an important part of every Passover discussion even though our discussion in this chapter centers on the grandfather, father and sons. Here the Torah is discussing important issues related to the father and sons. The purpose is not to exclude mothers and daughters. It is done to address specific responsibilities of the father, sons, and grandsons. These responsibilities have to do with time and planning for Passover. Wives are constantly after their husbands weeks in advance of Passover regarding Passover preparations. Daughters are naturally drawn to Passover while sons are not.

It is each our responsibilities to participate, to listen and to learn. The Lord strengthened everything from Aleph to Tav of Pharaoh's heart and everything from Aleph to Tav of Pharaoh's servants heart for important reasons. The Lord displayed His Greatness through delivering us, the Jewish people, from Egypt. What happened in Egypt was not by mere chance, IT WAS DELIBERATE! And it was deliberate for specific reasons. One reason is for the father to relate the Passover story using every detail of how The Lord made a mockery of Egypt through miracles and powerful signs in delivering our relatives.

Ha Torah emphasizes the father's obligation to relate to each son on an individual basis because Ha Torah states, 'your son'. Ha Torah does not say Bih Nay Chehm meaning, sons. Ha Torah's intention is for each son to be taught on an individual basis. In Exodus 10.2

the word son is repeated three times. Ha Torah's intention is to emphasize each son's individuality. Ha Torah Recognizes that the personality of each son is different. Ha Torah is telling fathers to be aware of each son's individuality. Fathers are to reach out to each child individually to communicate the important message of deliverance to each son in a way that each son can both understand and receive it. Some translations fail to deliver the important message of individuality in their translation.

I place this instruction close to the front so fathers can begin discussing and relating the Passover Seder. Make this Passover year special, get each child involved.

Chapter Seven

Purchasing Passover Food

Several years ago when shopping for Passover and I was shocked to discover that grocery store after grocery store stocked Matzah **'NOT KOSHER FOR PASSOVER.'** Normally the Rebbetzin and I purchase Shmeurrah Matzah or participate in a Matzah bake at one of the local congregations. Everyone cannot do this. So it is very important to read every label when purchasing food for Passover.

Readers, there is a difference between Matzah and Passover Matzah. Passover is a time like no other time of the year. We are required to follow stricter Observances at Passover. Each item we purchase must be properly prepared in a kitchen / factory which is Pesadik. That means they use utensils that are kosher for Passover. That means they use only Passover approved products. This can be very confusing because the matzah we purchase throughout the year may not be KOSHER FOR PASSOVER.

This brings us to a two letter word, לא Loh, meaning 'no' or 'not'. לא Loh is the word that stands between what is Kosher for Passover and what is not Kosher for Passover!

There is another famous word with the same letters. אל El meaning God! The only difference is that the letters are reversed, the Aleph is first and the Lamid is second.

This is significant because words use The Letters א Aleph and ל Lamid. Their meaning is greatly different. This accentuates the confusion surrounding items that are kosher throughout the year but not kosher for Passover. God {El} says certain items are not {loh} kosher yet man has difficulty understanding this. Man has difficulty accepting this. Why? Because these same items are kosher the rest of the year...

Unfortunately that results are in grocery store after grocery store stocked with items NOT

KOSHER FOR PASSOVER! If Jews have difficulty understanding and accepting this, how do you think a non Jewish merchant will respond? How can all these items that are kosher throughout the year not be kosher at Passover?

Holy Reader, even though these situations are true, that does NOT {Loh} alter God's {El} Command regarding Passover. It is our responsibility to learn what is kosher for Passover and what is NOT KOSHER FOR PASSOVER! I cannot describe the feeling I am left with when observing store after store in and near Jewish communities stocking Matzah that is 'NOT KOSHER FOR PASSOVER!' The implication is clear! Who cares? Who cares enough to explain there is a difference? Who understands the difference?

Reader, let's review some of the basics. Do we understand the meaning of kashrus?

Let's review what kosher is.

The Bible states that only certain animals, birds and fish are kosher. These creatures must give their lives by a prescribed method that sanctifies God's Name. Then they must be rabbinically inspected, they must pass the inspection and be sealed by a mashgiach, sometimes two or three. Then they are shipped to their place of purchase where another mashgiach inspects their hecksher[20] and accepts or rejects the product based upon a variety of kashrus laws. In Colorado of all the fast food places, take outs, delivery and restaurants, only two are certified kosher for the members of our communities to eat at. PERIOD!

According to our sages there are three categories of food: Meat, Dairy and Parve. As a result we have three sets of dishes, silverware, pots and pans, etc. Ha Torah forbids us to mix meat and dairy products as well as their containers, etc. One may prepare parve foods in meat dishes. When parve foods are prepared

---

20 A Hecksher is a symbol that certifies the product has Rabbinical supervision and is kosher. There are levels of Rabbinical Supervision. Some levels are not accepted do to a number of reasons. One should consult the community Rav to determine what symbols are accepted.

in meat dishes they become like the meat. They may not be eaten with dairy foods. The same is true for dairy. When a parve food is prepared in dairy cookware that dish becomes dairy and must not be consumed with meat. If one desires to consume a parve dish with both meat and milk that dish must be prepared in parve cookware with parve utensils. The item must be stored in parve containers and served with parve forks spoons etc.

Dear Reader, we have a reserved area in our home where we store Passover dishes, pots and pans etc. They are cleaned placed in plastic then placed in fresh boxes. The boxes are sealed then placed in plastic again. The Passover boxes are stored in our pantry on shelves until the following Passover.

As we get closer to Passover we will need to make purchases of dishes, glasses, cookware, etc. This can be expensive. This is why we begin discussing Passover now while there is still some time to plan, save and prepare.

When Revi and I celebrated our first Passover together we were overwhelmed by what we needed. We needed so much. Much of what we owned in our kitchen was not kosher for Passover. We felt like crying... We felt depressed... We felt angry at all these requirements... Why? We were poor. We could not afford to purchase all that we needed. At that time, much of the Passover items that we owned were inexpensive pots and pan sets. That was it.

Readers, Passover is the head of the Jewish year! Passover is the most elevated time in terms of food. Jews use their very best dish sets during these eight days... The special dishes are ONLY used eight days. What is a young couple raised in a not so kosher setting supposed to do?. Here is what we did.

We determined that each year before Passover we would purchase one or two nice items to add to our Pesadic set. This is what we did. Our first year we purchased a crock pot. Now we had the least expensive pots and pan set from K Mart and their cheapest crock pot... That Passover we used plasticware. We got by... We did the same for the next few years until things began to change for us.. During the next couple of years we caught several nice sales for Farberware cookware... pots and pans... utensils, etc. A friend purchased a full set of beautiful glasses for us at about the same time.

Dear Reader, each of us begins where we are. We do the best we can and go from there. REMEMBER after purchasing dishes, pots, pans they will need to be kashered in the mikvah before being used. Revi and I take our things to the lake out back to kosher them. It is fed by a natural spring. There we open the boxes and remove all labels. After we remove all labels we place one item at a time in either a new fishing net or a laundry basket. We then lower the new item into the water until it is completely immersed, until 100% of the item is covered by water. Then we say, 'Blessed are you Ad-noy, King of the universe, who has sanctified us with His commandments and who has commanded us to immerse our vessels.'

We only say the blessing once. We say The Blessing in Hebrew but it is fine to recite the blessing in any language. The Creator understands. We recite this blessing over the first item we immerse but we intend for this blessing to apply to everything we need to immerse.

Readers, this is how we kasher items. Please keep in mind that one can only kasher new items... When we do this we are separating out dishes to HaShem for holy foods and holy purposes.

How are you coming on your housecleaning??

Chapter Eight

Selling, Searching And Burning Chometz

72 Hours Before Passover

We begin this chapter one day before Passover begins. Most of our Passover shopping should be winding down by this time. Our house cleaning should be wrapped up. I trust your Passover shopping was successful. As Passover approaches there are a number of important areas we must focus on.

Selling Chametz

Among The People of Israel there are those who purchase and sell chametz at Passover time. Buying and selling chometz begins about a week before Passover. ONE DOES NOT HAVE TO BE A RABBI to complete these transactions. But one does have to know what they are doing because many Jews may be depending upon their accuracy! If you are in or near a Jewish Community the area Rav normally handles the sale of chometz. If you are not close to a Jewish Community there are many online services to sell chometz. Some rabbium require a power of attorney to handle the sale of chametz. Yet most will accept a verbal request even on Erev Pesach. Do not wait until Erev Passover. handle your Chometz now!

Still it is best to state one's intention in writing to the individual they desire to sell their chametz to. Now this can be quite technical but it doesn't have to be.

Below are two forms. Form One is signed by the individual selling your chametz. This individual is acting as your agent. Form Two is a Delegation of Power of Attorney authorizing him to sell your chametz.

Form One
I, the undersigned, do hereby sell all manner of leavened bread and food products mixed with leaven and anything which is suspected of having leaven by our sages. I also sell or rent all areas where leavened bread or any leavened

product is found including storage areas and vessels that are used in preparation and storage of leaven. I direct my representative to sell or rent for me the above goods to someone other than B'nei Yisroel with this legal instrument, and with any other acts designed to transfer title recognized in Torah halacha and the law of the land from this point in time prior to the deadline for selling leavened bread, with an absolute sale, in accordance with all details contained in the attached sales document. We hereby sign this instrument on this day _____at _____.

Form Two
To all let it be known that I, the undersigned, fully empower and permit Rabbi _____ to act in my place and stead and in my behalf to sell all chametz possessed by me whether known or unknown as defined by Ha Torah and Rabbinic law {e.g. chametz, doubt of chametz, and all kinds of chametz mixtures}. Also chametz hardened and adhered to pans, pots, and any item used in cooking or storage of chametz or chametz mixtures and all

kinds of live animals that have been eating chametz or chametz mixtures thereof, especially in the premises located at

_____

_____and

elsewhere.

Rabbi _____ has the full right to sell and to lease by transactions, as he deems fit and proper and for such time which he believes necessary in accordance with all detailed terms and detailed forms as explained in the general authorization contracts which have been given this year to Rabbi _____ to sell the chametz.

This general authorization is made a part of this agreement. Also do I hereby give the said Rabbi _____ full power and authority to appoint in his stead with full power to sell and to lease as provided herein. The above given power is in conformity with all Torah, Rabbinical regulations and laws and also in accordance with the laws of the state of (STATE) and of the United States of

America. And to this I hereby affix my signature on this _____ day of Nisan in the year 5763.

Signature_____

Address_____
_____ City_____

Normally when one requests their Rav to act as their representative they make a contribution at that time...

We are one Day from when Passover begins. The traditional search for chometz begins after evening prayers tonight.

בְּדִיקַת חַמֵץ
Bih Dee Kat Chometz
Searching for Chametz
On the evening prior to the first seder B'nei Yisroel searches for chametz by candlelight using a feather and a wooden spoon. Many homes hide chametz wrapped in foil. In our home we do not follow this practice. Instead,

we recite the blessing Bi Dee Kaht Chaw Maytz, then check certain areas that could have chametz and that could have been forgotten like:
- all trash containers
- vacuum bag
- briefcases
- lunch boxes
- purses
- replace old toothbrushes with new

On The day leading up to the first Seder Meal at sunrise The First born begin fasting.

Taanit Bechorim
Fast of the Firstborn
From sunrise until sunset the child who is firstborn of a father or mother normally fasts as an expression of thanks for HaShem's Deliverance of the firstborn of B'nei Yisroel in and during the tenth and final plague.

On the way to morning prayers we make a run to a local dumpster to remove the final bags storing chametz.

Burning Chametz

Immediately after morning prayers we burn our last chometz. This is symbolic. We set aside a small amount of chametz that we save for the purpose of burning with fire. When we burn this chametz we say, 'Any chametz that is in my possession which I did or did not recognize, whether I did or did not see, whether I did or did not remove, shall be as if it does not exist and shall become ownerless like the dust of the ground.'

Chapter Nine

Haggadahs And Jewish Tradition

The Lord said to Moshe, 'Go to Pharaoh for I have made his heart stubborn and the heart of his servants... [Why?]...for the purpose of establishing a sign of these [great miracles that I performed] amidst [The Children of Israel]. And for the [explicit] purpose that you [carefully] recount [these great miracles] in the ears of your children and your children's children, [especially] how I made a mockery of Egypt with great signs and how I ostracized them that you know that I am The Lord.' Exodus 10:1, 2

The Holy Scriptures Teaches us that we are to learn about Passover from our parents. Our children are to learn about Passover from us and from our parents. This is the Torah method of continuing Judaism from one generation to the next generation. We call this TRADITION!

In addition this instruction teaches us that The Lord established a signal or a sign. That sign was the ten plagues, the Sea of Reeds splitting, The People of Israel crossing the sea on dry ground without even one casualty, and Pharaoh's army drowning in the Sea of Reeds. The Lord Performed these great miracles for us, The Children of Israel.

In addition The Holy Scriptures Teaches us we are to carefully recount these great miracles. Why do we need to recount these great miracles? Why do we need to be careful in recounting them? SO THAT EACH OF US WILL KNOW WITHOUT QUESTION THAT 'HE IS THE LORD!'

So now we arrive at a most important point. That point is the breakdown in our tradition. How can a Jew from an assimilated family carefully recount what was not passed down? What can a Jew recount from generations of assimilation? Holy Reader, one can see from this that assimilation is a most dreadful problem attacking our future. It is for this very reason that The Lord Established these great miracles. That is why Ha Torah records the story of our deliverance. This is why we call the first evening's Passover meal and the second evening's Passover meal the first Passover seder and the second Passover seder. The word 'seder' means order. There is an order to recounting the story of Passover! We use a Passover Haggadah to carefully recount the story of Passover. Haggadah means telling. The Haggadah was written for those of us who have this huge black hole of assimilation as part of our past. Our great grandfathers of many generations ago wrote stories recounting the miracles of Passover for us, their distant grandchildren. We can observe this mitzvah of learning, of teaching, of recounting through the use of a Passover Haggadah. We can restore what was lost to us through generations of assimilation.

Holy Reader, the Passover seder is a most special meal that is to be lavished. Revi and I reserve our very best for Passover. Our finest china, our finest gold rim glasses, our finest silverware, our best stainless steel cookware etc. WHY ?? Why reserve our very best for just eight days of the year? Again, Dear Reader, as we gaze on some of these very special pieces in our china cabinet throughout the year it is a powerful reminder of Passover. It is a reminder of the miracles. It is a reminder of The Lord's command to carefully recount His great signs!

Revi and I have with such love and pleasure carefully, meticulously added fine items to our Passover table. We both come from assimilated pasts so for us it is such a joy each year to restore a little of what was lost over generations of assimilation. We are not wealthy in the sense of being able to purchase the finest items in one Passover. In our own methodical way we continue on the path of replacing what was lost, forgotten or discarded... And for this we thank The Lord!!

One of the first and most important additions to our seder table was a book about 9' wide and 12' long. This book has about 60 pages most

of which are illustrated drawings all in color. I am making reference to the Passover Haggadah. What would a seder be like without a Passover Haggadah? The one that the Belk family uses is published by Artscroll. It is the Illustrated Youth Haggadah with the complete text, simplified translation and comments. It is available online at:
http://www.artscroll.com/haggadahs.html

We use this Haggadah because it is well-organized. The pictures keep the children interested. The stories with commentary are very good. Everything is covered! However you should find the haggadah that is right for you. The above link will provide you with many choices of which all are from a reputable publisher.

A friend mentioned that on one year they did not use there favorite haggadah. Some relatives visited and wanted to use their Passover Haggadah. IT WAS A MISTAKE! A sincere mistake. It did not carefully recount our deliverance from Egypt. He said it lacked recounting in the fullest sense.

Remember all the struggle and house cleaning and meal preparation it took to get to Passover. Enjoy The Seder. Take time to enjoy the Seder.! How much time? The Passover seder begins around 8:30 pm. Few families conclude their seder until after 2:00 am. A few families stay up the entire night sharing Passover stories then say morning prayers at daybreak. The point is that one should take enough time to carefully cover every detail!

For weeks we plan and prepare for Passover. Why rush through the seder? Invite those who will enrich and be enriched through the joy of Passover. We mention the point of the Haggadah because one should have time to get out and investigate what Haggadah they will select for the Passover seder...

God willing in the next lesson we will discuss special items on the Passover Seder Table..

Chapter Ten

The Seder Plate

The Seder Table is adorned differently that other high holidays. First many items will be missing like The Challah Board, Knife, Challah Cover and Challah. Certain drinks that often accompany a meal like whiskey, vodka and beer will also be missing. Foods used like bread, chicken, fish and meat will be missing. Products containing "B.R.O.W.S." {barely, rye, oats, wheat and/or spelt} will be missing. In many homes corn, beans and rice will also be gone. So Pesach ushers in life, house and menu changes.

When we look at the seder table we will notice the finest china, glassware, silverware and serving ware sitting on top of a beautiful Pesach tablecloth. We will also observe Elijah's cup, for the Prophet Elijah, the Afikomen bag, a haggadah at each setting, the seder plate, salt water, Avie's kittel,[21] and cushions and pillows on all the chairs for the family and guests to lean on.

The seder plate has six divisions. Various rabbium state the proper order for each item on the seder plate. We will not go through each order because the order is based on many different customs. The seder plate we are using follows the following custom. After our Holy Temple was destroyed the Sages ordained that the Pesach seder table should contain two cooked foods, one of meat - which is the Zih Roh Ah representing the Passover sacrifice and the other one a roasted egg representing the Karbon The Festival Sacrifice which was offered when The Holy Temple was in existence.

Zih Roh Ah
The Shank Bone
One may use a chicken thigh bone or neck in place of the lambs shank bone. We call it Zih

---

21 The Kittel is a white garment worn by Jewish men who are married. The kittel reminds us of the day of our death. Jewish men are buried in their kittel.

Roh Ah {arm} to remind us of HaShem's outstretched arm in Egypt, used to deliver us, B'nai Yisroel from slavery. The shank bone, chicken thigh bone or neck is roasted in the oven until dark. See Exodus 12.8,9 and Deuteronomy16.7.

Bay Tzaw
The Hard Boiled egg
The hard boiled egg is either boiled over a fire or roasted in an oven. Bay Tzaw is Aramaic for Beiah {desire}. Beiah represents the Jewish slave's desire for HaShem to redeem them with an outstretched arm. The egg should be prepared hours before Erev Passover is to begin. Then one must eat it on the first day of Passover. The egg is a food eaten by mourners.

Maw Rur {bitter herbs}
The purpose of the maw rur is to remind us of how bitter slavery is. We are to remember how bitter our lives were in Egypt! Any one of several vegetables may be used as maw rur. Normally romaine lettuce or horseradish are used. Endive is not used because it is not the

same as in the Mideast region.

Hah Roh Seht
Is a mixture of ground nuts, fruits, spices and wine. Hah roh seht is normally a mixture of apples, walnuts, pecans or almonds, filberts, cinnamon or ginger, honey and sweet red wine served as 'mortar 'between the matzahs that is thick like mortar which was used between the bricks in Egypt.

Apples symbolize the apple trees Hebrew women laid under outside the gates of the cities in Mitzriam. Hebrew women went to the apple groves to bear their children. This was away from the evil taskmasters and anyone who could hear their cries.

Almonds symbolize the quickness by which HaShem Delivered B'nai Yisroel. The almond ripens fast representing this quickness.

Filberts / hazelnuts are used because Israel is compared to a garden of hazelnuts. Song of Solomon 6:11

Ginger symbolizes the mortar used in Mitzriam

Red wine symbolizes the blood.

Cahr Pahs / Celery or Parsley
Raw potatoes, radishes, onions or root may also be used as Karpas. The Karpas is dipped in either salt water, oil or vinegar. This represents our sweat, our tears, from slavery in Egypt.

Chah Zeh Reht / Horseradish
The chah zeh reht is normally horseradish which is used between the matzahs like a sandwich.

Chapter Eleven

Wine

First let's discuss wine. In Yiddishkeit there is a term known as Yayin Nesekh {wine handled by a heathen}. Originally Yayin Nesekh meant wine offered to idols. Today among the observant Jews it means wine handled by non Jews. Our sages forbid Jews to drink Yayin Nesekh. Now there is a great bit of disparity to this rabbinical ruling. For example, the Committee on Law and Standards of the Rabbinical Assembly {Conservative Judaism} ruled that automated wine manufacturing is kosher. They accept wine whereby the grapes are not picked or supervised by Jews. They accept wine which is not touched by human hands... has no human contact from the time it is fed into vats until it is sealed in bottles.

Strict observance requires that rabbinic supervision be present throughout the entire process and that the wine be labeled by a recognized kashrus organization. There are many symbols that are of stricter standards. However in honesty I must say my own experience in working with some of the so-called strict kashrus organizations was disappointing. So what I am saying based upon my own experience is that when possible, pick your own grapes and learn how to produce your own wine according to Ha Torah. My Zayde {grandfather}, may he rest in peace, was a winemaker. Revi and I are also winemakers. Now that does not mean that we do not purchase wine. We do.

Wine contacted by an idolator at any stage of its preparation is the basis to prohibit its consumption by a Jew. Why? Anything used by an idolator in ceremonies is prohibited for Jewish consumption. To make this easy for us who desire to be careful, strict observance differentiates between kosher and non kosher wine. Kosher wine has two categories. First is "not mevushal" which means it has not been cooked or boiled. It is acceptable for a non Jew to handle the bottle as long as the seal is intact.

Once the seal is broken non Jews are prohibited access. The second category is "mevushal." The presumption is that wine boiled after pressing is not associated with pagan use. The term that includes this process is "mevushal." This wine may be handled by non Jews even after it has been opened.

At Passover red wine is preferred because red wine is considered superior to white wine. Only red wine may be used for drink offerings. Our Sages point to Proverbs 23.31 where Ha Tenach States that one should not gaze on red wine. The fact that one should not gaze implies Holiness with regard to red wine which white wine does not have. This implies that proper wine must be red. Hence, only red wine should be used for Pesach. Red wine is symbolic of the blood which flowed when Pharaoh murdered innocent Jewish children. However, the use of red wine is not a Torah requirement. I like red wine but often am forced to be moderate because of its effects on joints, etc. Yet red wine is good for other ailments. In addition, a quality kosher for Passover red wine might not be available. In such a situation white wine is fine. Thousands of years ago it was customary to dilute wine because of its potency. Today we do not dilute wine because one can use even kosher grape juice or wine.

When one is preparing to drink four or, in some homes, five cups of wine, each of these factors should be considered and the host should be consulted in advance if one is concerned.

Chapter Twelve

The Four Cups Of Wine

Our sages teach that all are bound to drink the four cups, men, women, and children, according to R. Judah. Yet other sages point out that children are not required to drink four cups of wine because this mitzvah was not ordained for them. However, it is considered a mitzvah to give them a cup of wine. The child fulfills this mitzvah by taking a mouthful. The amount therefore differs for children... One should be careful when giving wine to children.. {Mishnah Berurah 472:46,47.

Now I would like to point out that Kosher for Pesach Grape Juice is acceptable as wine. So it is not necessary for one or one's children to become intoxicated. Now one must ask, How much wine is required of an adult? It is preferable for an adult to drink the entire cup of wine yet it is acceptable to drink most of an average cup. The Metsudah Kitzur Shulchan Aruch sights views ranging from 2.9 fluid ounces to 5.1 fluid ounces. Then one must drink most of their cup. Most of 5.1 fluid ounces would be at least 2.9 fluid ounces. So the answer is 2.9 fluid ounces.

One may ask, Why four cups of wine? Our sages teach that the four cups of wine correspond to the following:

For each cup of wine we express gratitude and joy to HaShem.

Cup One
I will bring you out, expresses the excessive oppression, tyranny and sufferings in Egypt ended.

Cup Two
I will rescue you, expresses the end to bondage and captivity ended.

Cup Three

I will redeem you, expresses the deliverance from Mitzriam was through HaShem's outstretched arm and through His great judgments against Egypt.

Cup Four
I will take you to Myself as a people, expresses that HaShem became our God and we became the people chosen to Observe Ha Torah.

The Cup of Elijah The Prophet
At each Passover Seder table there is a place setting and a cup for the prophet Elijah. Ha Tenach requires that Elijah the prophet return to earth as the forerunner of Moshiach / The Messiah. Elijah represents the greatest deliverance and freedom of B'nei Yisroel which is yet to come!! Elijah the prophet symbolizes the Fifth Cup which is not drunk because of B'nei Yisroel's long exile. The fifth cup represents our awareness and our desire for fulfillment. We await El Ee Yah Hu - Ha Na Vee to return and to drink the fifth cup! This fifth cup, known as Elijah's cup, represents the

ingathering of Jewish exiles from the four corners of the earth, the reestablishment of Jewish sovereignty of Eretz Yisroel.

Chapter Thirteen

Telling The Passover Story

Holy Reader, one can only imagine what it must have been like for those living in Egypt during the months, weeks, days and even hours leading up to the tenth and final plague when The Children of Israel would be driven out. Yet observance of Passover {Passover} requires us to reach back, to revisit that day, to renew our connection with our past and to teach our children about all the glory and miracles of Passover. Telling the story of Passover is a major mitzvah. The story of Passover shares how The Lord Delivered The Children of Israel from Egypt with a Strong Hand. The Lord Heard The Children of Israel's cry of death, suffering and oppression. The Lord Called Moshe to go to Pharaoh and say, *Send My people out* [of Egypt] *so they may celebrate a festival to Me in the wilderness.* Exodus 5.1 Pharaoh refused. The Lord Answered

Pharaoh's refusal with a series of ten plagues.

Plague 1 All the water for the Egyptian people turned to blood.

Plague 2 Frogs covered the entire land of Egypt.

Plague 3 The dust of Egypt turned to lice.

Plague 4 Bears, birds of prey, lions, panthers, mice, serpents, scorpions, wolves, etc. invaded the land of Egypt. They did not invade the land of Goshen where The Children of Israel lived. A Jewish woman was carrying four of her Egyptian master's children to the marketplace. She was panting and moaning under the heavy load of four children. When she returned to her master's home, her master asked where his children were. She replied. A lion took one child. A bear grabbed one child. A wolf took the third child and a panther the fourth.

Plague 5 A heavy disease struck down the

livestock of Egypt.

Plague 6 The Egyptian people were struck with body boils.

Plague 7 Large hailstones with fire crushed and burned the land and the people of Egypt.

Plague 8 Swarms of Locusts covered the land, the fields and trees of Egypt consuming all vegetation of Egypt except the land of Goshen.

Plague 9 Darkness that was so thick the people of Egypt were frozen in place for three days.

Plague 10 The firstborn of man and beast in Egypt without lamb's blood on their doorposts died. After the tenth plague Pharaoh and the people of Egypt drove The Children of Israel from Egypt. The Children of Israel had only 18 minutes to prepare to leave. In this short time they mixed flour with water and baked matzos. The matzos lasted for three days.

Rabbi Yose the Galilean, Rabbi Eliezer and

Rabbi Akiva were fulfilling the mitzvah of remembering and expressing gratitude about The Lord's deliverance of The Children of Israel {the children of Israel} from Egypt {Egypt}. They were discussing the 10 plagues The Lord struck the Egyptians with.

Rabbi Yose asked, 'How do we figure that the Egyptians were cursed with 10 plagues in Egypt but with 50 plagues at the Sea? He points out that The Bible states that Pharaoh's magicians said to him that the plagues in Egypt were the finger of God. The plagues at the sea, however, the Torah describes as the great *hand* of God which He laid upon the Egyptians. How many plagues did God strike the Egyptians with using His finger? Ten! Then when He used His whole hand, there were 50 plagues!

Rabbi Eliezer asked, 'How do we figure that every plague that the Alm-ghty struck the Egyptians with in Egypt was equal to 4 plagues?' He explains that The Bible states that God sent His fierce anger upon them:

1)wrath, 2)fury, 3)trouble and 4)a band of emissaries of evil. He concluded that 4 plagues in each x 10 plagues = 40 plagues. Therefore, at the sea, they were struck with 4 plagues in each x 50 plagues = 200 plagues!

Rabbi Akiva asked, 'How does one figure that each plague the Holy One, Blessed is He, struck the Egyptians with in Egypt was equal to 5 plagues?' He points out that The Bible relates that God sent His 1)fierce anger upon them: 2)wrath, 3)fury, 4)trouble and 5)a band of emissaries of evil. He concluded that 5 plagues in each x 10 plagues = 50 plagues. Therefore, at the sea, they were struck with 5 plagues in each x 50 plagues = 250 plagues!

So Readers, from this story we can see that the destruction afflicted upon the Egyptians was very great. Yet it was not as great as God's deliverance.

Chapter Fourteen

How To Count the Omer

The evening following the first seder meal we begin counting the Omer as Commanded in Leviticus 23:15 - 16. We strongly recommend that one obtain and follow a guide for counting the Omer. Counting the Omer has to be done correctly. The Bible Journeys Calendar includes a guide for Counting The Omer. Each Day during The Counting of The Omer is listed with the number for that evening. Counting The Omer is a Mitzvot[22] of Ha Torah. The People of Israel are required to count the Omer. We are required to count The Day and The Week[23].

Our calender is a guide to counting the Omer. We frame the count as follows, 'At Dark Count'. In actuality we count after evening

---

22 A מִצְוָה Mitzvah (singular) or Mitzvot (plural) means Command.
23 Rabbi A. Y. Kahan The Taryag Mitzvot (Brooklyn, N.Y. Keser Torah Publications 1987, 1988) p 190

prayers which are said after dark. One should say: *Blessed Are You The Lord our God, King of the universe, Who Has Sanctified us / Separated us with His Commandments and Has Commanded us regarding the counting of the Omer.* At this point, say, *Today is the ___ day of the Omer.*

What is the Omer? An עֹמֶר Oh Mehr is a measurement of barley sheaves brought on Passover Day as a sacrifice offering. Ha Torah Says, 'You shall count from The Day of Rest' which is in reference to Passover Day. The Omer of barley is brought each Day during the forty-nine Days. On The Fiftieth Day an offering of wheat is brought.

Again, it is VERY IMPORTANT to count the Omer correctly! It is very easy to lose track of what the Omer count is, so use this calendar or another guide to stay on track. One should not count the Omer until after nightfall. When counting the Omer one should say the above blessing.

When counting The Omer it is preferable to count the Omer in Hebrew, but if one does not know Hebrew, it is fine to count in one's own language. One must be extremely careful during this time period not to count the day aside from saying the blessing! For example, if one were to inquire what the Omer count would be for the coming day, our Sages suggest that one should say the following, for example: *Yesterday was the ____ day of the Omer...* or something like y*esterday was the 5th day of the Omer and tomorrow is the 7th day of the Omer.*

If one were to slip and say the Omer count before night this is considered counting the Omer without saying the blessing. As a result one cannot say the blessing when counting the Omer that night. It is preferable to say the blessing of the Omer in a minyan, A group of 10 Jewish men but it is acceptable to say it by oneself also.

If one has questions regarding the Omer, they should speak with the halachic authority of their community.

If one forgets to count the Omer at night, it is acceptable to count during the day but without a blessing. You may still recite the blessing on the nights that follow. If you forgot to count all day, however, you count without a blessing on the nights that follow. So one should be extremely careful to count the Omer within the correct time frame so they can say the blessing.

There is much more to counting the Omer than what I have stated here in this brief discussion. One of the great beauties of counting the Omer is that each day represents a different level of the 49 spheres (Sefirot). And each week represents a different level of the 7 spheres(Sefirot), in accordance with Jewish mysticism. One should study the Sefirot period, i.e. the 49 days of the counting of the Omer with a qualified authority. Each Day is supposed to be a step of greater purity and freedom from improper living. The fiftieth Day represents the Giving of The Torah and The Ten Commandments on Mt Sinai. I discuss this in greater length in my book My Bible Journal.

During the first 33 Days of Counting The Omer we are mournful because disease killed thousands of Rabbi Akiva's students. It is a custom of many Jews not marry during these days or have joyful celebrations. One does not cut their hair on nails.

Lag B' Omer is the thirty- three days of The Omer. Our custom is after Lag B'Omer the restrictions are lifted because Rabbi Akiva's disciples ceased from dying.

There are different customs regarding Lag B'Omer. Most of The People of Israel follow the custom of the community they live in.

Chapter Fifteen
The Passover Offering

The Passover Offering is a point of considerable dispute among The People of Israel and Christians. We are not going to discuss the dispute here. I discuss the dispute in my book, The Last Six Days Of Jesus Life On Earth.

The Passover Offering was for the purpose of saving the firstborn child. The only ones saved by The Passover Offering were the First Born Children. The Passover Lamb or Kid had NOTHING to do with forgiveness of sin.

The Egyptians had many gods. The lamb was one of their gods. So the Lord God Commanded that The People of Israel take a lamb or a kid on the tenth of The First Month and tie the lamb or kid to their bed post.[24] The Egyptians saw tens of thousands of the men of Israel parading lambs down the streets of Egypt. The action has many sides. The Egyptians learned that their gods were about to be killed. They were very angry! Slaves were about to kill their gods. On the other hand the slaves, i.e. The People of Israel had this new courage. The courage was POWERFUL! The Jews were about to kill thousands of the Egyptian gods. How did this feel to those who were enslaved? Freedom was in sight! Parading the lambs down the streets of Egypt required bravery! Proclaiming the lambs and the kids would be killed took even more courage and faith in The Promise of The Lord God.

The Lamb was tied to the bed post from the tenth of the month until the evening of the fourteenth of the month, about four days. The lamb was cute. The lamb was tiny and fluffy.

---

[24] Rabbi Moshe Weissman, The Midrash Says Sh'mos (Brooklyn, New York: Benei Yakov Publications 1980), p. 96

The children fell in love with the lamb. Then the lamb was killed. The lamb was NOT a sin offering. Think of the impact! The lamb died just like the firstborn of Egypt. The lamb was killed to save the firstborn. The lambs blood on the door post was a sign to the Egyptians! Four days ago we took a spotless pure little fluffy lamb. We walked it down our streets. We tied the lamb to our bed post. Then four days later we killed your god as we said we were going to do. We put your god's blood on our doorpost. We Observed the instructions of The Lord God of Israel. Killing the lamb was the height of rebellion against the gods of Egypt. Killing the lamb showed the loyalty of the Hebrew slaves to The Lord God and to Moses. Thousands upon thousands of first borns died at the mid of night in Egypt because the Egyptian people would not do as The Lord God Commanded. There was one Command. There was one time of death, i.e. Mid of night. There was only one method to protect the firstborn.

After the death of the first born Egyptian children The People of Israel were freed. Anyone who had blood on their doorpost was quickly driven out of Egypt. Only the firstborn children in Egypt died. The firstborn children throughout the rest of the world were safe.

The blood of the lamb was not for forgiveness of sin. The blood of the lamb was to protect the firstborn. That's it!!

Exodus 12.3 - 29

Speak to all the congregation of Israel, saying, In the tenth day of this month they shall take every man a lamb, according to the house of their fathers, a lamb for a house; And if the household is too little for the lamb, let him and his neighbor next to his house take it according to the number of the souls; according to every man's eating shall you make your count for the lamb. Your lamb shall be without blemish, a male of the first year; you shall take it out from the sheep, or from the goats; And you shall keep it up until the fourteenth day of the same month; and the whole assembly of the congregation of Israel shall kill it in the evening. And they shall take of the blood, and strike it on the two side posts and on the upper door post of the houses, in which they shall eat it. And they shall eat the meat in that night, roast with fire, and unleavened bread; and with bitter herbs they shall eat it. Eat it not raw, nor boil with water, but roast it with fire; its head with its legs, and with its inner parts. And you shall let nothing of it remain until the morning; and that which remains of it until the morning you shall burn with fire. And thus shall you eat it; with your loins girded, your shoes on your feet, and your staff in your hand; and you shall eat it in haste; it is the Lord's Passover. For I will pass through the land of Egypt this night, and will strike all the firstborn in the land of Egypt, both man and beast; and against all the gods of Egypt I will execute judgment; I am the Lord. And the blood shall be to you for a sign upon the houses where you are; and when I see the blood, I will pass over you, and the plague shall not be upon you to destroy you, when I strike the land of Egypt. And this day shall be to you for a memorial; and you shall keep it a feast to the Lord throughout your generations; you shall keep it a feast by an ordinance forever. Seven days shall you eat unleavened bread; the first day you shall put away leaven out of your houses; for whoever eats leavened bread from the first day until the seventh day, that soul shall be cut off from Israel. And in the first day there shall be a holy convocation, and in the seventh day there shall be a holy convocation to you; no kind of work shall be done in them, save that which every man must eat, only that may be done by you. And you shall observe the Feast of Unleavened Bread; for in this same day have I brought your armies out of the land of Egypt; therefore shall you observe this day in your generations by an ordinance forever. In the first month, on the fourteenth day of the month at evening, you shall eat unleavened bread, until the twenty first day of the month at evening. Seven days shall there be no leaven found in your houses; for whoever eats that which is leavened, that soul shall be cut off from the congregation of

Israel, whether he is a stranger, or born in the land. You shall eat nothing leavened; in all your habitations shall you eat unleavened bread. Then Moses called for all the elders of Israel, and said to them, Draw out and take a lamb according to your families, and kill the Passover lamb. And you shall take a bunch of hyssop, and dip it in the blood that is in the basin, and strike the lintel and the two side posts with the blood that is in the basin; and none of you shall go out from the door of his house until the morning. For the Lord will pass through to strike the Egyptians; and when he sees the blood upon the lintel, and on the two side posts, the Lord will pass over the door, and will not let the destroyer come into your houses to strike you. And you shall observe this thing for an ordinance to you and to your sons forever. And it shall come to pass, when you come to the land which the Lord will give you, according as he has promised, that you shall keep this service. And it shall come to pass, when your children shall say to you, What do you mean by this service? That you shall say, It is the sacrifice of the Lord's

Passover, who passed over the houses of the people of Israel in Egypt, when he struck the Egyptians, and saved our houses. And the people bowed their heads and worshipped. And the people of Israel went away, and did as the Lord had commanded Moses and Aaron, so did they. And it came to pass, that at midnight the Lord struck all the firstborn in the land of Egypt, from the firstborn of Pharaoh who sat on his throne to the firstborn of the captive who was in the dungeon; and all the firstborn of cattle.

The Passover lamb was roasted. The lamb was consumed. Any part of the lamb that was not eaten by morning was burned by fire. The People ate the Passover Lamb in haste with their loins girded, their shoes on their feet and their staff in your hand. Ha Torah does not mention anything about packing bags or preparing food for their journey. Our Sages Teach that The People of Israel made Matzah, i.e. unleavened bread for their journey in less than eighteen minutes as they were rushing out of Egypt. The People of Israel spent the last eighteen minutes of their time in Egypt baking unleavened cakes before leaving Egypt. Does that seem unusual?

The People of Israel had several weeks to choose the right lamb but only minutes to prepare food for their journey. The People of Israel planned the slaughter for their Passover lamb and their Passover meal but not their journey into the wilderness. Ha Torah Informs us that all the men had to have a Brit Milah a circumcision before eating the Passover Lamb at the Passover meal.[25] If a man was not circumcised he could not eat the Passover Lamb.[26] He could not kill the Passover Lamb! Now we are beginning to see and to understand the far reaching impact of the Passover Lamb.

Before the Passover meal the people were instructed to borrow from their Egyptian

---
25 Exodus 12.43 - 51
26 Rabbi Moshe Weissman, The Midrash Says (Brooklyn, New York: Benei Yakov Publications 1980), p. 99 Moses and Joshua circumcised all the men, boys and converts.

neighbor jewels of silver and gold.[27] Not having the people prepare to leave was deliberate. The emphasis was on the establishment of The Passover sacrifice for The Lord, not the leaving from Egypt. So we did what The Lord Commanded first then the Lord God God Delivered us in haste from Egypt.

---

27 Exodus 11.1-4

Chapter Sixteen

The Four Questions

One of the very great traditions at the Pesach Seder is Mah Neesh Tah Nawh, 'Why is this night different from all other nights?' Traditionally Mah Neesh Tah Nawh is asked by the youngest child in the home. Mah Neesh Tah Nawh is a brief highlight of the very first Passover, designed to point out that on the same night we were both slaves and royalty. As slaves we eat Matzah and Marror. As royalty we recline on pillows, dip our food and have others pour our wine. We both remember and celebrate the many miracles that happened leading up to Passover and one each Passover afterwards.

Mah Neesh Tah Nawh is actually one very long question aimed at teaching our children and the child in all of us.. Why children? Ha Torah Teaches that children were murdered.[28]

---
28 Exodus 1.16 - 22

The children were the helpless. They were vulnerable to Pharaoh's evil decrees. Our sages teach that Pharaoh used to have Jewish babies killed just to bathe in their blood. Our sages also state that Jewish babies were smashed into the walls in place of bricks when The People of Israel did not make bricks fast enough. In our world today Jewish children are born into assimilated homes. Jewish children and non Jewish children are born to mixed marriages between Jews and non Jews where they learn little or nothing about Ha Torah and Judaism and where they unfortunately are taught about idolatry and false gods. Passover is intended to reach our children. Mah Neesh Tah Nawh is intended to personalize Passover for our children. We encourage our children to ask questions and to participate.

Our sages teach that there are four types of children that we must teach, the wise child who wants to learn, the evil child who considers Passover too much effort,[29] the simple child

---

[29] This shows he / she does believe in Ha Torah.

who does not understand anything about Pesach, and the child who does not even know how to ask questions. The four questions also represent four groups of adults. Each group requires a different approach. We teach everything to the wise child, even up to not eating after the Afikoman[30]. The evil child we rebuke. We personalize the message. We explain that HaShem did the miracles **for me** when I left Mitzriam. We involve the evil child. The simple child requires patience. We must take the time to patient. We lovingly and carefully go over the explanation and details of Passover. The child that does not know how to ask we teach how to ask. We teach them that HaShem did these miracles for me when I left Mitzriam.

We discuss the meaning of Passover. We share the story of Passover. We try to bring Passover to life.

---

30 The Afikoman is the Matzah dessert.

Chapter Seventeen

The Matzah Bake

I threw cotton balls on the Passover table when we talked about the hail and little plastic frogs for the plague of frogs. We use the kids Haggadah. We search the house for chomets with a candle and feather. We burn the chometz. It is all for the children. The children we have and the child in us. The steps to Passover are intended to bring powerful and wonderful meaning into our lives.

Years ago a friend invited me to participate in a matzah bake at a local congregation. It didn't seem all that exciting until he mentioned we would be learning with a great Rabbi. We drove to the Rabbi's office to learn more about the matzoh bake. We met with the Rabbi. He informed us that we would need to learn and review Ha Torah Mitzvot for Passover In preparation for the matzah bake. We agreed. We scheduled an appointment for the following week. We learned together right up until we began Baking Matzah's in the Mazah Factory. We learned that every stage from when the wheat was harvested up until we used the wheat for the Matzah Bake was supervised. The wheat was gathered, ground and bagged then placed in a secure moisture free and rodent free storage area. The storage area was locked and guarded. Observant Jews whom The Rabbi trusted would pick up several fifty pound bags of flour when they visited the east coast. They inspected the bags carefully. When they determined They were kosher for Passover they were packaged in preparation for shipping. They followed a particular procedure in transporting the flour. When they delivered the flour to our storage area we removed them from the shipping container and examined the exterior bags. When we determined they were 100 percent secure from any damage they were placed in our storage area and locked. Only the Rabbi had the key to the secured storage area. When it came time to gather water for the Matzah Bake we loaded a truck with with sealed boxes. We broke the seals when we reached the well. The boxes have clear one gallon glass jars. The well was about 800 feet deep. Each year we would go back to this well to draw water. The Rabbi's father, may his memory be for good, made arrangements for us to draw our Passover water from this well. We drew the water at a particular time of night on a particular day. We said a blessing, then began filling the glass jars. We repeated the words La Sham Matzah Mitzvot throughout the process. We were doing this in honor of the Commands regarding the Matzah.

The Matzah bake area was an especially secure area. Our pockets were empty. We wore white aprons etc. No food, drink etc. was permitted in the Matzah Bake area. There were lines of tables covered with fresh white heavy duty paper running about seventy feet from one end of the room to the other. On one end of the Matzah Factor a sanding station was set up. There were several tables with dozens of one inch thick dowels. The dowels were used used for rolling the matzah. We cleaned the dowels with fine sand paper. It was necessary for several individuals to constantly sand the dowel rollers after being used. They sanded the rollers until they were 100 percent free of everything. Being a sander was intense and difficult. The sanding station had a used roller area, a roller cleaning area and an area where clean rollers were placed. Every roller had to be entirely sanded after each Matzah bake.

To the left of the sanding station was a sterile stainless steel kitchen which was used to clean the Matzah perforators. After the matzahs were rolled they had to be perforated before being placed in the ovens. Every perforator had to be 100 percent cleaned before the next Mazah Bake could begin. One individual ran the perforate cleaning station.

To the left of the perforator cleaning station was the small matzah baking room. Inside the Mazah Baking room was a huge heavy duty floor to ceiling oven with special bricks inserted to greatly increase the heat. On each side of the oven area tables were set for the baked matzahs, wooden oven paddles and oven gloves. A special fan air intake drew the hot air to outside.

In front of the bake room were the perforating tables. Rolled matzahs were placed on the perforating tables, perforated then placed in the ovens. Normally the two most experienced individuals operated the Bake Room. This is where the Rabbi and one other individual worked. The perforating tables normally had two individuals.

To the left of the Oven room was the timer. The timer set the timing device on eighteen minutes exactly. When the mixer called time the timer would turn on the timing device. From that point on EVERYONE was on the clock.

To the left of the timer was the water room where the glass jars of well spring water were kept. Only one individual worked the water station. The water pourer measured the water into a special container and waited to be called by the matzah mixer.

To the left of the water room was the flour room. Only one individual worked in the flour room. The individual in the flour room was confined to that room. no wandering in and out. No liquids were permitted anywhere around the flour room / area. Inside of the flour room a table was set up to weigh the flour. The weighed flour was placed in a container.

In front of the water room and flour room was a special matzah mixing station where a stainless steel bowl was attached to a table base. When the matzah mixer called time the flour person would bring a container with the exact prescribed flour out from the flour room then pour the flour in the stainless steel mixing bowl. After the flour person returned to the flour room the water pourer would bring a container of water and begin pouring as the matzah mixer hand mixed the flour and water into dough. After pouring the water into the dough he / she would return to the water room. It was very important not to pour too much water into the flour because additional flour could not be added. The flour person could not come near any form of liquid.

To the left of the matzah mixing area were several tables where mixed matzah was divided. When the matzah mixer reached that perfect consistency, The stainless steel bowl was entirely cleaned of dough. Then the matzah mixer would take the dough to the mixing table to be divided and handed out to matzah rollers.

Individuals known as Matzah rollers would stand in line to receive a small portion of mixed dough. They would take the dough to their rolling area. Each individual was permitted to have ONLY one piece of dough at a time. After the dough was rolled it was taken to the perforating table. Then the roller lined up back in front of the matzah mixing table to receive another small portion of dough. At times dozens of holy rollers would line up to receive a small portion of matzah. Matzah is separated from all other bread. Matzah is regulated by strict Torah Observances. Matzah is holy bread. Individuals who roll matzahs are holy rollers. They are preforming a number of Observances by participating in a matzah bake.

When there were plenty of rollers on hand the process would immediately begin again. If there were two matzah mixers they would switch off mixing. Depending upon how well coordinated the process was it would be possible to process about four mixes of dough and bake them into matzahs within eighteen minutes.

After an eighteen minute matzah bake it was necessary to clean up. Clean up could take a half hour or longer. All stations had to be 100 percent clean before a new matzah bake could begin. All the paper was removed from the rolling tables. All the rolling dowels had to be sanded. The wooden oven paddles had to be sanded. The paper and boxes on the sanding station had to be removed. Then the paper had to be removed from the sanding station tables. All the perforators had to be cleaned. The perforator table covers had to be removed from the perforating station. The oven gloves had to be removed. The baked matzahs had to be inspected and stored outside of the Matzah Baking area. The table covers in the Matzah Baking Room had to be removed. The stainless steel bowls and basins had to be cleaned. All aprons had to be removed. the floors had to be swept. After all this was completed every station had to be inspected by The Rabbi or a qualified individual trained by the Rabbi. Once the extreme inspection was completed and everything was certified 100 percent clean then everyone would put on fresh clean aprons, hats etc. All the tables would be recovered with fresh paper. Then we could begin again.

If there were a small group of rollers present several hours may be required to prepare for a new matzah bake. We would do this every day but Sabbath for about three to four weeks. The Hebrew Day Schools, Hebrew Learning Centers and congregations would sign up for baking sessions. They would bake their own kosher for passover Matzahs which were certified by the Rabbi. It was wonderful to be part of this experience!!

It was midday on erev Passover. Everyone was dressed in suits and dresses. We were standing in the Matzah Factory just hours before Passover would begin. The Rabbi was decked out. He stood there tall in his long black silk coat with a fur strommal on his head. The Rebbie began to speak. It was like yesterday. He expressed his thanks for making the Matzah bake such a success. The Rebbie spoke of Messiah coming and each of us joining in Jerusalem next year. It was a powerful, tear rendering message. Then we began our final bake before Passover...

May each of us have a blessed Passover.

About The Author

Dr. Akiva Gamliel Belk

Jewish, Husband, Father, Step Father, Grandfather and Step Great Grandfather.

Graduate:
A.A. Long Beach City College,
B.A. Southern California Bible

Seminary:
M.A. Southern California Theological Seminary
D. Th. Southern California Theological Seminary
D. Th. Denver Charismatic Theological Seminary

Individual Study:
Rabbi Dovid Nusbaum,
Bais Medrash at Yeshiva Toras Chaim,
Ha Rav Mordicai Tewerski
Hornosteipler Rebbe,

GROUP STUDY:
RABBI YAAKOV MEYER, AISH DENVER
RABBI YISROEL ENGEL, DIRECTOR,
COLORADO CHABAD.

FOUNDER:
JEWISHPATH.ORG
JEWISHLINK.NET
7COMMANDS.COM
BNTI.US

DEAN OF JEWISH STUDIES
B'NAI NOACH TORAH INSTITUTE
BIBLICAL ONLINE STUDIES

AUTHOR OF VARIOUS BOOKS
BNTI.US/BOOKS.HTML

Books By Dr. Akiva Gamliel Belk

A Taste Of Gematria Genesis

Gematria Azer is the compilation of each weeks Parshat study for Bereisheit / Genesis for 2013. We dig deep into some subjects like What is The Creator's Revealed Light?, What is it Like to be Perfect? Is Prayer Important?, Who is my SoulMate?, What makes a man the perfect husband? and What are actions of love? There are relevant Gematrias that answer these questions. We discuss and explore them. A brief video based on the center question of each Chapter / Parshat is also available.

A Taste Of Gematria Exodus

We discuss subjects like How do we praise The Lord God? The Lord God Has Chosen the People of Israel to offer praise to Him. Everything that has flesh is to bless His Name. Everyone that has breath is to bless His Name. Each Chapter discusses a different question like: What is the Name of The Lord? What do we really need to know? *You will know that the earth belongs to The Lord... Can one be thankful enough? What is prophecy? Why do we Observe The Commands Of The Lord God... Why should we give?*

Eve Of Creation RESTORED

The Creator Has been so Merciful and Gracious to help me share valuable life restoring Words USING GEMATRIA for Husbands, Wives and family in my book entitled: Eve Of Creation - RESTORED. The focus of my book is on how to repair and improve oneself and one's relationships. Adam teaches us how to reverse poor choices and improve our lives. Eve Teaches us patience beyond imagination.

MY Bible Journal

My Bible Journal covers many gripping, enthralling subjects like a step by step journey from when the People of Israel left Egypt until they received The Ten Commandments about Fifty Days later. What events led to the destruction of the world in Noah's age and other subjects like these.

My Bible Journal shares Biblical and historical

information I gathered, compiled condensed, and prepared from decades of personal research. My book is an excellent source for understanding more about The Bible, Biblical History, and Jewish Observances. This is an excellent learning tool and a teaching tool. The information easy to follow and understand. My Bible Journal was written in conjuction with each years Bible Journey Calendar. They go hand in hand.

The Bible Journeys Calendar - 24 Months

The Bible Journeys Calender has many interesting journeys. Did you know that Moses twice fasted 40 Days, one immediately following the other. Actually Moses fasted between 122 - 123 Days. His fast ended on Yom Kippur when he came down from Mt Sinai with the second set of The Ten Commands on Two Stone Tablets.

When do The Six Days of Creating begin? How about the Ten Plagues The Lord God Brought on Egypt. When do they begin? When do they end.

When did Noah's Flood begin? How long did the

flood last? How long were the inhabitants on The ark? These historical events and the dates for many additional events are recorded in this new updated calendar. The Name for Each Weekly Parshat is listed along with the Weekly Reading. Each High Holy Day is listed along with related readings.

My Bible Journal was written in conjuction with each years Bible Journey Calendar.

The 2016 Bible Journeys Calendar - 16 Months

The 2016 Bible Journeys Calender began in September of 2015 and continues until December 31, 2016. The calendar includes the Name for each Weekly Parshat and High Holiday along with the Scripture Reading. Jewish and civil Holidays are listed. Many fascinating Bible journeys are listed and followed as they ocurred thousands of years ago, like the Six Days of Creating, the Ten Plagues in Egypt, Noah's Flood and much more. My Bible Journal was written in conjuction with each years Bible Journey Calendar.

The 2017 Bible Journeys Calendar - 16 Months

The 2017 Bible Journeys Calender begins in

September of 2016 and continues until December 31, 2017. The calendar includes the Name for each Weekly Parshat and High Holiday along with the Scripture Reading. Jewish and civil Holidays are listed. Many fascinating Bible journeys are listed and followed as they ocurred thousands of years ago, like the Six Days of Creating, the Ten Plagues in Egypt, Noah's Flood and much more. My Bible Journal was written in conjuction with each years Bible Journey Calendar.

Find The Hebrew Letter

Learning Hebrew is not difficult if one has an excellent guide that is not complicated. 'Find The Hebrew Letter' is a fun enjoyable way to learn and to retain what one has learned.

We focus on identifying The Hebrew Letters. That is it! The first step in Learning Hebrew begins with The Hebrew Letters.

It is amazing what can be understood by just learning 22 Letters. Our goal is to know The Hebrew Letters thoroughly. Open the door to a new exciting world. It is just amazing. Most anyone can learn 22 letters. Think about it. . .

Gematria And Mysticism IN GENESIS - I
The reader will be introduced to truths not discussed among the religions of the world. Hebrew in the Bible unveils answers to many mysteries. The entire Bible is founded upon Genesis, Exodus, Leviticus, Numbers and Deuteronomy and the truths that flow out of these five books is different than the rest of the Bible. Why? There is a system of Hebrew Letters with which each have a numerical value that have the power to reveal interesting and mystifying relationships within the Hebrew Letters, Words, Phrases etc. of the First Five Books. The cost of this book is a small investment for what the reader will learn.

Gematria And Mysticism IN GENESIS - I I
Book Two is a continuation of where Book One concluded. Book 2 covers Genesis Chapters 11 through 20.

Gematria And Mysticism IN GENESIS - I I I
Book Three continues where Book Two concluded.

Book Three covers Genesis Chapters 21 through 30.

The Jesus Probe

The Jesus Probe will require you to study and to research and to face Truth you have not been aware of. Can you handle Truth that challenges what you believe? Can you face Truth that collides with the doctrines of the Church?

Mysterious SIGNS Of The Torah in GENESIS

Mysterious SIGNS Of The Torah Revealed In GENESIS is an exploration of Biblical truths organized into the Weekly Parshat study of the Bible. Dr. Akiva Gamliel has been recording and referencing decades of study and research. He has gathered, compiled and organized years of discovery into this mystical book for us to learn, enjoy and share. Many years can pass between one discovery to another which forms a bridge between two discoveries. Revelations are the product of many bridges. Enclosed in this book are some of these special relationships.

Mysterious SIGNS Of The Torah in EXODUS

This is the second in a series of Five Books, God Willing. This book is deep, intense, inspiring and extremely interesting. Yet, it is easy to read and follow. Dr. Akiva Gamliel includes a Gematria Chart in the beginning of the book. Like each of Dr. Akiva Gamliel's Gematria books there are special Gematrias waiting for the Reader to discover. There is a special sweetness in sharing a Torah Gematria / Sign during a wonderful warm Friday Erev Shabbat meal or another occasion.

Mysterious SIGNS Of The Torah in LEVITICUS

This is the third in a series of Five Books, God Willing. This book is deep, intense, inspiring and extremely interesting. Yet, it is easy to read and follow.

Time And Gematria In Deuteronomy

Time and Gematria In Deuteronomy points in the direction of the great war our Prophets foretold. My book unfolds connections to The End of Days. It may be surprising to learn that Moses spoke a great deal about The End of Days in Deuteronomy. We dig deeper into the hidden through Gematria revelations. Today, there are similarities to the Year 2488 From Creation when The People of Israel began their conquest of The Land of Canaan. Then the land of Canaan was occupied by vile, wicked, sinful nations. Today the land of Israel is in part occupied by people who teach their children to murder The People of Israel God Forbid!

America has made a deal with Iran to allow nuclear progression that opens the door for atomic weapons. Russia has entered Syria. Our enemies are stabbing innocent, God Fearing, law abiding Jews.

All of this is pointing to The Messiah coming soon. The Lion will lay down with the Lamb. We will study war no more. We will live in peace. We will discuss these subjects and much more.

God's Plan From The Beginning

Does God exist? Yes! Does God have an universal plan? Yes! Does God know me? Yes! Does God know I exist? Yes! How do I fit into God's Plan? We discuss sin, salvation, death hell, eternal life, life after death and many more interesting issues.

Would You Like To Be Jewish ?
Many readers would like to know what it is like to be Jewish. Some have tried to learn what it is like to be Jewish. Some visited with a Rabbi who may have said, something like this, 'Why do you want to convert? Why do you want to be Jewish? We don't do conversions in Judaism.' You ended up walking away disappointed, angered, exasperated, annoyed and very dissatisfied. This book answers questions about what Jews believe in a way you will not forget.

Would You Like To Be Jewish 2 ?
This is a continuation of the first book, Would You Like To Be Jewish. In this book we learn that God has always had a plan, even before the beginning of Creation. We learn how God Teaches us to repent when we fail and when we make mistakes. We discover God is very understanding, compassionate and forgiving. We share about fallen angels, Satan, hell and how to live eternally with God.

PASSOVER
The Last Six Days of Jesus Life On Earth

The Gospel Writers each offer a different perspective of Jesus last six days on Earth. They differ some. I offer my own perspective as a Jew that has been on both sides of this discussion. If you are a Christian... If you believe in Jesus this book will be very challenging. I started on this Journey almost 30 years ago with a desire to give my Baptist Congregation a historical view of Jesus last six days on earth. Since then I have returned to Judaism. I share some of the untold stories and fill in some of the blank pages... My journey can be of great help to you if you discern there are problems with the story the story the Christian Writers tell of Jesus last six days on earth.

A Sincere Journey Ends Without Jesus

This is an autobiography of my spiritual journey. My journey did not begin with the goal of returning to Judaism. My journey began with a desire to give my Baptist Congregation a historical view of Jesus last six days on earth. My journey has been very challenging for me. If you read this book and if you walk in my footsteps, believing in Jesus will become a challenge for you also. The difference is I am on this side of the journey now. I have returned to Judaism. The journey of my life can be of great help to you if you discern there are problems with the story the New Testament story of Jesus.

www.ingramcontent.com/pod-product-compliance
Lightning Source LLC
Chambersburg PA
CBHW071726090426
42738CB00009B/1889